Bow Wow*

The Somewhat Comprehensive Book of Dog Names

SPOT

Faye Passow

* Dogs will ask for it by name.

First Edition
09 08 07 06 05   5 4 3 2 1

Published by
Gibbs Smith, Publisher
P.O. Box 667
Layton, Utah 84041

Orders: 1.800.748.5439
www.gibbs-smith.com

Designed by Faye Passow
Printed and bound in the United States of America

Library of Congress Cataloging-in-Publication Data

Passow, Faye.
  Bowwow : the somewhat comprehensive book of dog names / by Faye Passow.—
1st ed.
      p. cm.
  ISBN 1-58685-736-3
  1. Dogs—Names. I. Title.

SF422.3.P368 2005
929.9'7—dc22

2004023355

Dawg Names

Biff	Laddie
Bosco	Lady
Boxer	Pal
Bruno	Rover
Buster	Scottie
Butch	Shep
Fido	Spot

bone

bowl

bits

bite

Human Names

Amos	Marsden	Belle	Marvel
Barney	Max	Betty	Mavis
Baxter	Moe	Clovis	Midge
Billy	Muldoon	Doris	Molly
Clark	Pete	Dot	Nicki
Dell	Rex	Gracie	Opal
Doyle	Riley	Hazel	Pat
Elroy	Rufus	Larue	Peg
Fritz	Sholto	Libby	Stella
Jake	Thody	Madge	Tess
Jarvis	Toby	Marge	Trixie
Lloyd	Wally	Marlis	Vie

Pure Breds

Barkley	Percy	Dorothia
Beauregard	Phelps	Eudora
Chompton	Pomeroy	Henrietta
Commodore	Rolf	Lilith
Digby	Shelbourne	Mercedes
Giles	Sumner	Miranda
Hippollyte	Wadsworth	Phillipa
Humphrey	Beatrice	Portia
Huntley	Deirdra	Sybilline
Nesbitt	Desdimonia	Wilhelmina

Victorian

Alice	Albert
Bertha	Alonzo
Bessie	Cecil
Charlotte	Edward
Clara	George
Dora	Gideon
Eliza	Hugo
Louisa	Jasper
Lucy	Jules
Mae	Vernon
Polly	Willie

DORA

Characters from Dickens

Blimber
Chuzzlewit
Crup
Heep
Jiniwin
Jorkins
Kenwigs
Lirriper
Markleham
Merrylegs
Miggs
Noggs
Nupkins

Orlick
Pawkins
Peerybingle
Phiz
Pip
Quilip
Smike
Snubbin
Swiveller
Toodle
Wilfer

LEADERS

Big Chief	Majestic
Captain	Major
Champ	Paladin
Colonel	Prince
Contessa	Princess
Count	Queeny
Dame	Sarge
Deputy	Scout
Duchess	Sentinel
Duke	Texas Ranger
Inspector	Topper
King	Valiant

HISTORY'S BRAVEST!

Agamemnon	Hannibal
Alcazar	Hercules
Ali Baba	Napoleon
Amenhotep	Odin
Atlas	Procyon
Charlemagne	Rob Roy
Cleopatra	Samson
Cochise	Sirius
Geronimo	Sitting Bull
Gilgamesh	Sulliman
Gorgon	Tecumseh

"RESCUE CHIHUAHUAS"

Sweets

Baby
Beauty
Bliss
Bubbles
Candy
Cookie
Cuddles
Cutie Pie
Honey Bunch
Lambkins
Lover Boy

Lovums
Peaches
Precious
Pretty
Sparkles
Sugar
Sunny
Sweetie
Treasure
Twinkles
Valentine

Good Dogs

Buddy	Loyal
Charm	Lucky
Dandy	Magic
Destiny	Sassy
Happy	Trusty
Honor	
Keeper	

Mutts

Biff	Iggy	Schmitty
Buzz	Knute	Smedley
Bud	Lester	Slick
Chuck	Mutt	Slug
Clem	Mange	Schuster
Chumly	Mug	Skunk
Curr	Puke	Thug
Dewey	Pugsley	Tubby
Dexter	Rascal	Weasel
Dwayne	Rocko	Willard
Goober	Seymour	Wilbur
Heimy		Whimpy

pound

pounce

puddle

pest

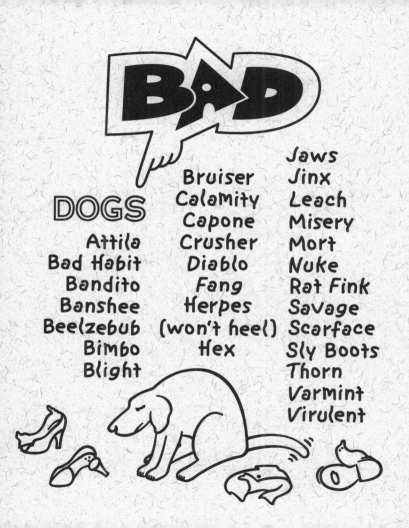

WORLDLY DOGS

Below Normal	Misty
Blizzard	North Wind
Dense Fog	Shadow
Drizzle	Snowy
Echo	Storm
Eclipse	Thunder
Granite	Tornado
Hurricane	Whirlwind
Scattered Showers	

Out of This World!

Angel	Luna
Apollo	Moonglow
Aurora	Neptune
Booster	Nova
Brown Dwarf	Orbit
Celestine	Ozone
Circe	Rocket
Cosmos	Sputnik
Jupiter	Stardust

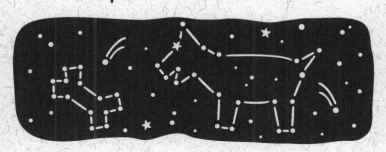

COLORS

Blacky	Red
Brownie	Rosy
Blondie	Ruby
Cocoa	Pinky
Goldie	Violet
Rusty	Blue
Whitey	Olive

DOUBLE DOG

Bébé	Ju Ju
Bobo	Kiki
Chi Chi	Lulu
Coco	Mimi
Dede	Pepe
Fifi	Toto
Gi Gi	Tou Tou
Jo Jo	Yo Yo

Biscuit   Gum Drop   Pickles
Biz Scotty   Jelly Roll   Pork Chop
Brandy   Juice   Pumpkin
Butterscotch   Marshmallow   Ruta Beggar
Chowder   Meat   Schnitzel
Dumpling   Niblet   Scrapple
Gherkin   Noodles   Taffy
Ginger Snap   Peanut   Tater
Grits   Pepper   Turnip

MILK

PET ME

Cuddles   Fuzzy   Shaggy
Curly   Mr. Softy   Snuggles
Dusty   Mopsy   Tufty
Floppy   Plush   Velvetina
Flossy   Ruggles   Waggles
Fluffy   Wooly Boy

FLOWER POWER

BUD	PETUNIA
CLOVER	POPPY
DAFFODIL	POSEY
HYACINTH	ROSE
IRIS	SQUASH BLOSSOM
MARIGOLD	TRAILING ARBUTUS
MERTENSIA	TULIP
NASTURTIUM	VIOLET
PANSY	WILD GINGER

Rhymin' Simon

Fuddy-Duddy   Itsy-Bitsy
Fuzzle-Muzzle   Jelly-Belly
Fuzzy-Wuzzy   Lovey-Dovey
Harum-Scarum   Namby-Pamby
Heebie-Jeebie   Rosie-Posie
Higgledy-Piggledy   Rufus-Gufus
Hocus-Pocus   Silly-Billy
Hurly-Burly   Ugly-Bugly
Ipsy-Pipsy   Woolly-Bully

Secondhand Rover

Bingo	Checkers	Scooter
Blood	Domino	Scraps
Bomber	Dust Mop	Slippers
Boomerang	Hoover	Sprocket
Bows	Knuckles	Staples
Brillo	Legs	Stitch
Bubbles	Paws	Tumbleweed
Buckles	Polyester	Velcro
Bullet	Rags	Yard Butt
Buttons		Whiskers

PAIRS

Prince & Frog	Arthur & Murray
Banjo & Earplug	Cramps & Motrin
Pudding & Mousse	Jello & The Blob
JuJu A & JuJu B	Peas & Carrots
Sparky & Plug	Chad & Jeremy

Dan'l Boone & The Bahr
Hot Dog & Curly Fries
Jimmy & Sprinkles
Meatloaf & Green Beans
Pizza Man & Cable Guy
Lazy Boy & Barkalounger
Square Peg & Round Holden

Handles

Augie the Swamp Angel
Collapsible Mabel
Dewey Decibel   Dieter the Eater
Drool Hand Luke   Elvis the Pelvis
Fast Freddie   Flora Fair
Heedless Johnny   Inky Boy
Ivan the Terrier
Marcus the Carcass
Monty the Snake Shaker
Nancy Fancy   Not Spot
Nosey Parker   Odious Thelodious
Parker the Marker
Puddler Jim   Sid Vicious
Tim the Thief   Wet Nose Willie

Action Figures

Boomerang	Gabby	Slinger
Chase	Gimpy	Snapper
Chewy	Grumpy	Snipes
Crash	Maverick	Snitch
Dasher	Nipsy	Snuggles
Digger	Pacer	Sparky
Dodger	Pokey	Spike
Dribbles	Ruggles	Swifty
Flash	Scamp	Tatters
Flip	Scooter	Thrasher
Fowler	Skeeter	Troubles
Fumbles	Skippy	Zippy

DICTIONARY DOG

Abnormous Winthrop
Anurous Nancy
Chuffy Muffy
Curr Cullion
Cumbrous Kirkpatrick
Dirk the Doughty
Edwina the Edacious
Fred Foozler
Gina Gentilesse
Idiosyncratic Ida
Impavid Paul
Innominate Dawg
Lolloping Lois

Malapert Barbie
Mansuetudinal Matilda
Phonate Pearson
Harry the Pilose
Rimpled Riley
Roland Rudesby
Reg the Rugose
Spalpeen Maureen
Todd the Sparger
Ted the Temerarious
Tarcus Tetrapod
Ululant Ulana

STRAIGHT FROM THE
PHONE BOOK

ALLICEE, Rex
ARDUG, Holes
ARGON, Kibbles
BARKER, Constance
BEG-MOORE, Euwanti
BISQUETZ, Cumfor
BITTEN, F. Lea
BONESWELL, Barry
CHEWEN, Boots A.
CHOWDOWN, Snarfs

GOOD, Upton O.
LOAFER, Justa
KIBBLEDORFER, Otto
PARADOXUND, Moe & Zoë
POSTMAN, Chomp Z.
SANSZEEBARK, Gilbert
TREATS, Willeatum
TUPICK, Bone
YARDS, I. Mark
WIZZ, Golly G.

BRRING! BRRING! ARRRF! ARRRF!

AIR FRESHENER
PAHLEESE!

Dusty	Slobber
Greasy	Snuffles
Grubby	Snuffy
Itchy	Sooty
Muddy	Stinky
Noisome Nel	Straggles
Puddles	Thunder Bum
Rancid Ralph	Tinkles
Scratchy	Wheezer
Scruffy	Whiffer

SHAPELY

DOGS

Baby Dumpling
Big Galoot
Blimpy
Butterball
Chubby
Dainty Hippo
Jumbo
Lumpy
Midget
Pee Wee
Runt
Sasquatch
Shorty
Slim
Smidgeon
Squirt
Stumpy
Tinker Toy

Strange (but true)

Coricopat	Mowgli
Darton	Octo
Dwina	Oppo
Krexpel	Quoxo
Loth	Timpango
Lozette	Toomaii
Lozo	Tox
Ludo	Zoltan
Misnak	Zwollo